The Phoenix Living Poets

A SENSE OF BEING

The Phoenix Living Poets

★

A SENSE OF
BEING

by

John Horder

CHATTO AND WINDUS

THE HOGARTH PRESS

1968

Published by
Chatto and Windus Ltd
with The Hogarth Press Ltd
42 William IV Street
London WC2
*
Clarke, Irwin and Co Ltd
Toronto

SBN 7011 1324 3

Printed in Great Britain by
William Lewis (Printers) Limited
Cardiff

For the two Gabriels,
GABRIEL FIELDING
and
GABRIEL FALKENBERG,
with love

Acknowledgements are made to *Ambit*, *The Cambridge Review*, *Extra Verse*, *New Christian*, *New Poems 1963* (the P.E.N. anthology), *The Observer*, *Outposts*, *The Poetry Review*, *The Scotsman*, *The Spectator*, *The Tablet*, *The Transatlantic Review*, *Tribune* and *Twentieth Century*: also to the B.B.C. Light Programme for "Not Far Off" and "The White Blackbird": and to Penguin Books and Dr. R. D. Laing for permission to include a "found-poem" from *The Politics of Experience and the Birds of Paradise*.

The author wishes to thank Michael Szasz for his help with Attila Jozsef's poem "Mother".

Ten of these poems appeared in *The Child Walks Around Its Own Grave* (Giles Gordon, 1966).

During 1966 two lesser awards for poetry were made to the author by the Arts Council of Great Britain.

Contents

THE MINDFUL

It is that territory
Where the mindful fear to tread,
Scouring their way for rational posts
Trees to grasp or gates to lean on,
Suspecting my inclination
As I cycle down Sidgwick Avenue at night
Of turning the leaves of the plane trees
Into pieces of paper sculpture,
Tresses of gold supported by wire.

The mindful shiver and hover
Casting care against sadness,
Afraid of the Romantic nightmare
They pause on the word, grasping its meaning
Syntactically yet hardly with feeling.
The point between mind and feeling
Has yet to be found.
One must go beyond the word.

THE SICK IMAGE OF MY FATHER FADES

The sick image of my father fades.
When I was three he used to take me
Tied up in a sack to the cliff's edge
And threaten to throw me over. The wind
Was ghastly, and his hands shook with terror.
I whimpered like a fretful dog. Fear
Stole over me, and I shrieked and screamed.

My father said, shall I break your legs
Before throwing you over? You should then land
On the sand without the sudden crunch crunch
Of breaking bones. I looked up at him, pleading.
Then he would laugh out loud like a normal man,
And let me clamber back onto his back, so that I forgot
The sheer drop from the cliff's edge, just for a moment.

THE MEASURE OF THEIR FEAR

Hanging under those long, long moments
When I'm quite sure I'm going to die,
Or pass out at any moment, or lie for ever
In a tiny wrinkled box, alone,
While the rain silently rots away at the wood,

I wonder at the owls, romantic and melancholy,
Locked up in their private myth, desperate as poets
In their inability to communicate,
Taking up uneasy posts in the dark,
Wings tremulous, yet who would know it,
Knowing the measure of their fear, yet quite mastering it.

THE FEELING WAS THE SAME

The dark, crisp, black houses off Pemberton's Crescent
Brought back my childhood. Inside, everything was still
And dead. The literary man pondered a little, like a servant,
Handing me a cup of tea and a couple of dry biscuits.

Upstairs his wife lay ill with the 'flu. This disturbed me,
Bringing back memories of my mother's final illness. I waited,
Looked up at the grandfather clock stuck at one o'clock,
And remembered how I had remained stuck for so many years

In another room. Not Victorian even, like this one, with its
Plum-coloured chairs and row upon row of volumes of poetry,
But the feeling of death had been the same. The literary man
Showed me to the door and outside, in the darkness, I wondered
what had hit me.

THE CHILD WALKS AROUND ITS OWN GRAVE

The child walks around its own grave.
He's surprised to see his own body
Laid out, several feet, below ground level.
One of its hands begins to spread out of fear's grip.

He's afraid. Strange that any life should have been left
At all, after so long. That whole body had grown numb
For so long, that the pain, when first felt,
Had been almost more than he (or it) could bear.

To rest in death can be protective.
He'd sheltered in his own dead body
For over eighteen years. The child's cries, in that time,
Had hardly been heard. Now he's overwhelmed by the noise.

TOMBS AND WOMBS

Tombs
Are very much like
Wombs:
They're both places
Where there's very little room
In which to stretch your feet.

MY MUSE LAST NIGHT

My muse visited me last night.
Left a terrible trail of blood
On the tips of the spiked railings
Outside my house.
Really, you'd think she'd be more considerate.
Made a most filthy mess for all the neighbours to see.

CRAZY JANE AND YEATS

I am dead now.
Dead.
Dead right up to the fingertips.
Crazy Jane is playing about with Yeats in heaven.
God! How she can *squeal*. Such a noise!
Crazy Jane
Is dead again.
Gosh, I'm dead too.
Past the point of shock and terror.
Inanimate.
My God, Yeats is rising up in the sky
In a cloud, just like Jehovah.
I always knew he had it in him.
And Crazy Jane's
Dropped dead again.
Anything might happen.

LITTLE WILLIE

Little Willie was a most beautiful child.
His mother didn't love him quite enough.
This is a dilemma
The whole world knows *something* of.

After she'd died when he was three
He desperately tried to get her back;
Over a period of thirty years
He went through a series of patent cures.

He moved to a health resort and started a course in meditation,
And even tried to get to know a number of highly unsuitable women.
All to no avail. His mother wouldn't come back from the dead
However hard he tried.

MOTHER

after the original by Attila Jozsef

For a week now, in fits and starts,
I have been thinking of one thing only — my mother.
With creaking basket set against her lap
She went up to the loft
Went busily.

I still held that most precious thing of all — my integrity.
I raged, I roared
I bawled all over the place.
Insisted on her leaving the clothes behind
And take *me* up to the loft with her!

She just went
Spreading out the clothes in complete silence
Did not scold
Or even look down at me.
The bright colours of her clothes swished and swirled.

But now I would not so much as snivel or skulk
And now it's much too late for any of that.
I still see her for the giant figure she is.
She is the sky and her grey hairs hover over the blue
Dissolving at once by a stroke of very fine brushwork.

BEFORE MEETING MY MAKER

What would you do
Asked the fashionable woman journalist
If you knew
You were going to die tomorrow?
Yes, just what would you do?

Most of us would prefer
To go straight to the stake
Without warning. But with hours, minutes, seconds
To fill in?
Surely the pleasure of life would wear rather thin.

Depends on how much pleasure
You can pack into a minute.
I'd have lots of cups of Lyons Red Label Tea,
So that I'd want to pee, all afternoon.
Lots of bread and jam, followed

By slices of the most succulent ham.
I'd take the most delicious girl for a long country walk,
And then, without warning, pluck her like a stalk.
Lying back on our backs we'd look up into the skies
And we'd talk. God! How we would talk.

BALLAD

The cormorant nests
On a heap of broken images
By the sea shore

I lie inside you
Rosy Lee, Rosy Lee,
I lie inside you

The images dart in and out
Like shrimps
From the inside of your net

Rest your head, beside me
Rosy Lee Rosy Lee,
Rest your head, beside me

You knew it all
With your yellow sideburns
And your leather oilskin jeans

Wait for me, Rosy Lee, Rosy Lee,
Wait for me,
Rosy Lee

I can't explain exactly what happened.
The girl was too far out at sea
And she drowned.

A SENSE OF BEING

There is nothing in me to assure me of my being.
That is why I so often think
About my heart beating.
Nothing to do with the fear of it stopping.
It's just it's so hard to imagine it — beating —
Just as it's hard to imagine that I derive from something
That actually *works*. Something that lives and breathes.
Something that has a sense of its own being.
Oh, it's so very hard to imagine these things,
And I've always been told that I was imaginative by nature.

Imagine: a tree has roots: it knows where it springs from.
We have parents. But the orphan and the murderer have one
     thing in common.
Something vital in each of them has been wiped out.
It's hard to explain exactly what. It's something
A word or a glance from a parent may have set into motion
Or not. It's not that this gives a child a sense of itself
Just like that. Nothing as simple as that.
But it can be the basis. Something to start from, something
     that grows
And will eventually determine who and what he's to be
Or not to be, as the case may be. Whether he is, or is not.

PLANTING A BODY

'Shall we fill up the hole with gravel?
'The hole, I mean, that is inside your mind.'
'Which one?' you ask petulantly.
'The large one,' I reply, impatient, 'the void, where
'The conscious is always trying to meet up
'With the unconscious. It's difficult,' I agree,
'Bloody difficult. Most people spend most of their lives
'Trying to fill up the space with a body, anybody,
'Just so that someone's there.
'Planting a body, they call this.

'You don't get it? Well, a good father or mother
'Can help you to fill up the hole that's inside you.
'Otherwise this whole business of planting a body,
'Anybody, becomes a necessity. Doesn't much matter who,
'For most people, just so long as they make some attempt
'To fill it up. Damned important to pretend it's not there.
'You still don't understand. Well, if someone's to hand
'They can help you from falling down it. Or pull
'You up out, or help make you more aware that it's there.
'Don't worry. Fill it up with gravel. It's far less trouble.'

A SHAME

I took a hold of my shame
And had a good look at it.
My shame at being.
My shame took a hold of me
And made me more aware
That I was there.

I was forced to examine it
The reasons for it.
A desire for intercourse with Mum
Was how it had all begun.
And whyever not
Except that she was not

In relation to me.
Therefore I was not.
My agony of mind
At being so confined.
My agony of soul
And where she should have been, a gaping hole.

THE MEASURE OF OUR GUILT

The measure of our guilt
Is very great. It stretches round our waists
Like a thick belt, a notch or two too tight.
You cannot hear the breathing
For all the heaving.

The measure of my guilt
Is stretched very tight.
It never leaves me very far out of sight.
It descends
And perpetually winds.

IN A TIME WHEN I WAS NOTHING

In a time when I was nothing
I was strangely surprised to see
My name in *The Times Literary Supplement* .

In a time when I was nothing
There was an emptiness both inside and outside of me
And I felt no thing substantially.

In a time when I was nothing
It was most difficult to separate past from present
And the present moment held no sway.

In a time when I was nothing
There seemed no end to this state of non-being
The bottom had been kicked away from everything.

After a long time being nothing
There came at long last a dim realisation
That one day I might eventually become something.

In the time when I was no one
There was simply nothing left to give anyone
And I found myself cut off from everyone.

In the time when I was no one
I knew no man, no woman
And that was when my sense of self began.

SPLIT – IN TWO

'I want your spirit,' said the woman,
'As well as your body.
'It is hell
'To be one without the other.'

'I haven't found my spirit yet,' said the man,
'And, moreover, I have no means of finding it.
'It is lost. Lost. Somewhere amongst all the debris.
'Besides which, modern life gives me no will for the task.'

'Find it,' said the woman,
'You are not you without it.
'You have no centre.'

'I have no will to the task,' said the man.

'You have no will,' said the woman.

THE WOMAN OF SPEW

Here we have a woman with a diseased mind.
The colour of spew.
Toffee — layers of toffee — lie in the place of her brain.
I meet her.
I am enveloped in sponge cake.
She is now a patient in the local lunatic asylum.
She should not do this to a man.
Contact, the mere meeting her, is repulsive.
Gooey, stodgey, the ooze, all the mess
Of what one meets up with. Nothing substantial,
No backbone. There is nothing there at all.
It is terrifying.
In the text books she goes
By the name of a woman.
There are only vague traces of her womanhood left.
I am not fit to meet such a demented imbecile.
I am not fit to bypass the layer upon layer of meringue
And not notice precisely what is happening.
It is frightening.
Terrifying.
There is nothing to come up against
The flesh has no real substance
There is no real spirit to infuse it
I loathe flesh that does not beget
A fire beneath, a fire within.

What have they done to man
Just what have they done to man.
They have ruined him.
He doesn't exist.
And in his place one finds

Time and time again
Where there should have been a man or woman
Only a squelchy mess.
These are facts we are in no position to dismiss.
Only confess.

THE STONE AGE BABY

From the moment of birth
When the stone age baby
Confronts the twentieth century
The baby is subjected to
These forces of violence
Called love,
As its mother and father have been
And their parents and their parents before them.
These forces are mainly concerned
With destroying most of its potentialities.
This enterprise is on the whole successful.
By the time the new human being is fifteen or so
We are left with a being like ourselves.
A half-crazed creature
More or less adjusted
To a mad world.
This is normality in our present age.

from R.D.Laing's
*The Politics of Experience
and the Bird of Paradise.*

THE CURATES

How impeccably well-dressed they are
These curates!
This one's whole body
Is spruced up in a sort of corset.
The expression on his face, contorted.

At what cost to himself and to others
Does he spend his whole life suppressing his vital energies.
At what a terrible cost!

EVERYMAN'S VIETNAM

Our whole lives are designed as means of escape
From the psychic forces that are deep down within.
We do anything rather than reckon with them.

Rather naively, we make call after call
Upon the telephone, in order to try exorcise them.
These forces which if submerged, first malinger, spit out,
                              then wear our selves thin.

We cram our lives full to the brim with work.
We come home late, too tired even to speak to our wives.
We get drunk, which only makes our ulcers more peptic,

And still these forces won't leave us alone.
Still they will never allow us a moment of rest.
Still we give them no real means of expression.

We don't reckon with these forces.
They are demons.
They will run us to the grave

Unless we turn them to the good.
We underestimate their power.
Most of the time, we don't even acknowledge that
                              they're there.

More fool us.

THE WHITE BLACKBIRD

The white blackbird
Suddenly flies out
Of its black box.

Death will occur
Like that
Sudden and sharp

And no looking back.
God lies subtly
At the sky's rim

Just out of sight.
The white blackbird approaches
Its black outline still visible

In all the white light.
It is all right.

Not an execution
But a homecoming.

It takes some time for the truth to dawn.

AN OLD MAN

An old man
High up
On a park bench
Takes stock of his soul.
It grows.

As he grows older
There is nothing else
For him left to do
Except to grow his soul.
He's forced *in* on himself.

He's doing, —
What he's postponed doing, —
What most of us postpone doing, —
For most of our working lives.
The excuse, always WORK,

Never fear of the unknown.
As it grows he is
No longer afraid to die.
He'd always been so terribly afraid
Of death. It had never been very far out of mind.

What an effort it had always been
To keep such thoughts at bay.
Suddenly he had emerged
Into the light of day.
It wasn't that the darkness
No longer existed.

It had merely lost its power to frighten.

NOT FAR OFF

Eternity is not far off:
On a clear day
I feel it to be
Just out of sight.

The folly of men
Is their purposefully ignoring
What is so painfully obvious
On a clear day.

BEFORE THE WORLD BEGAN

to Stevie Smith

I can well imagine God vegetating
Before the world began.
Poor old thing!
Can you imagine it
All that love, bottled up inside him
And no means of expression.

What a state to be in!
All that highly-charged energy
That goes to make up a truly living sexuality, which is love.
And no outlet.
No possible outlet.
What an aweful state to be in!

To know what to do with it.
Somehow, to be rid of it.
The wonder of it,
But oh, the folly of it!
And then, —that most frightful moment of all
After the Fall.

The defeat.
After man, his particular creation
Had been killed off in the very prime of his condition
And something of himself had been killed off in the process.
What could he do about it?
What could he possibly do

Except start off all over again
And somehow become that wounded creature himself.
You know the rest of the story.
It is quite, quite extraordinary.
We forget what it took him in terms of will
And strength and (let's face the full force of the word) of
     sacrifice

To send us his son.
The son he had loved all along
Most of all, and couldn't bear to be parted from
For one moment. For one single moment.
He was desperate. Utterly desperate.
Lucky for us he got over it

So great was his desire that each of us
Each single one of us, should be
As we had originally been intended to be, whole.
All the many millions he had let issue forth
Out of a love that came dangerously close most of the time
     to wrath.
People forget all this at their peril.
And beauty, like love, once seen, is terrible. Utterly terrible.

EL GRECO'S 'BURIAL OF COUNT ORGAZ'

to Edward Lucie-Smith

The Count's soul ascends into heaven
In the form of sanctified sperm —
Or an ectoplasm, if you prefer that word.
This is more important than either the solicitations of the
    men on earth,
Their infinite concern, or the divine intervention
Of either St. Stephen or of St. Augustine.

At the foot of the soul, grasping its thighs
Lies a woman. Naturally she doesn't want to let it go.
Is she the Count's mother? Perhaps. I don't know.
Somehow she is acting as the arbiter.
We are reminded that our essence
While on earth, was conceived by a woman

More so than at any other moment at the moment of death.
She is there, solid as earth.
There is nothing more she can do.
It remains for the soul to slip from this earth by itself.
It has to make its own way.
Judgement lies ahead of it

Divine judgement.
In this part of the picture we are suspended at that moment
    of time
When the ectoplasm has still to make its own way
To a judgement that will inevitably winkle out
In the twinkling of an eye, all that it has been
On earth, all that it is, can be.

There is no fear. None at all.
This reduction of the soul to its pure essence
Is full of violence
At the same time full of tenderness.
This is either what makes it or breaks it
Either in heaven or on earth.

It is our capacity for being brutally tender that is being tested
At this moment. That is why Christ's judgement of each of us,
Of each single one of us,
Is at the same time full of love as well as of wrath.
These qualities may have been muffled in us while on earth
Through fear. We have to be brought back to what we are.

Cordoba,
September 1966

NOT A FRACTION OF

I am not a fraction of
What I am meant to be
In the divine pity
And therein lies the tragedy.

COMING CLEAN

Cleanly uproot
A bulb
From the ground.

Slide it out
Of the adequately moist
Earth.

It will come clean
Without any roots
Dragging it down.

But some souls, more tied down
Find greater difficulty
Departing this earth.

LOVE POEM

I put a heavy burden on my love for you
With all my suffering I do not think I'll see it through
You know, I think, I'm terrified of love as of you.

You challenge all that I am, my love for you.
Part of me, the worst part, does not want to see it through
Right now, I'm torn apart by thought of losing you.

I cannot help myself; cannot help loving you
The eternal part's blocked up in both me and you
Repressed — this is what makes yours and my pain ring true.

You see, eternal beauty, once caught sight of, must come
                                                    through.
I am as scared of it as I am of you.
Unless we give our selves to it, we'll not come through.